THE INCLUSION MINDSET

Based on *Beyond Discomfort* by
Nadia Nagamootoo

First published in Great Britain by Practical Inspiration Publishing, 2026

© Nadia Nagamootoo and Practical Inspiration Publishing, 2026

The moral rights of the author have been asserted

ISBN 978-1-78860-901-2 (paperback)
      978-1-78860-902-9 (ebook)

All rights reserved. This book, or any portion thereof, may not be reproduced without the express written permission of the publisher.

Every effort has been made to trace copyright holders and to obtain their permission for the use of copyright material. The publisher apologizes for any errors or omissions and would be grateful if notified of any corrections that should be incorporated in future reprints or editions of this book.

EU GPSR representative: LOGOS EUROPE, 9 rue Nicolas Poussin, LA ROCHELLE 17000, France Contact@logoseurope.eu.

Want to bulk-buy copies of this book for your team and colleagues? We can customize the content and co-brand *The Inclusion Mindset* to suit your business's needs.

Please email info@practicalinspiration.com for more details.

Contents

Series introduction iv
Introduction 1
Day 1: Why inclusion feels hard 8
Day 2: The lens we see through 17
Day 3: The four Ways of Being 24
Day 4: The Disconcerted Leader 33
Day 5: The Proof-Seeker 43
Day 6: The Cheerleader 51
Day 7: Leading Beyond Discomfort 59
Day 8: Building an inclusive culture 67
Day 9: Facing the future of work 78
Day 10: Your inclusion mindset journey 85
Conclusion 94
Endnotes 96

Series introduction

Welcome to *6-Minute Smarts*!

This is a series of very short books with one simple purpose: to introduce you to ideas that can make life and work better, and to give you time and space to think about how those ideas might apply to *your* life and work.

Each book introduces you to ten powerful ideas, but ideas on their own are useless – that's why each idea is followed by self-coaching questions to help you work out the 'so what?' for you in just six minutes of exploratory writing. What's exploratory writing? It's the kind of writing you do just for yourself, fast and free, without worrying what anyone else thinks. It's not just about getting ideas out of your head and onto paper where you can see them; it's about finding new connections and insights as you write. This is where the magic happens.

Whatever you're facing, there's a *6-Minute Smarts* book just for you. And once you've learned how to coach yourself through a new idea, you'll be smarter for life.

Find out more...

Introduction

When my husband and I decided to get married, we had a long discussion about what our surname was going to be. My family name is Nagamootoo and his family name is Smith. I am first-generation UK-born with a Mauritian heritage. I am proud of this heritage as much as I am proud to be British. Not only does my surname signal this important part of my identity, but I am also fortunate that it is pretty unique and therefore memorable.

I didn't have anything against being a Smith, but even in my late twenties I knew I wanted the type of career that would have a public profile, and so using any leverage I could get to stand out from the crowd would be helpful. It's also worth bearing in mind that by then I already had plenty of experience of being overlooked and underestimated due to my petite stature, ethnic background and hereditary youthful looks (for which I am most thankful now I am in my forties!). I learned to compensate for these hurdles of physicality by ensuring I was one of the first to speak when meeting new people, reeling off my credentials by way of introduction and injecting confidence in my voice.

Anyway, back to the surname debate. As you can imagine, this wasn't the type of quick, easily solved conversation you might have to, say, decide what colour to paint the living room. This was the type of complex, meaty and not so clear-cut conversation that pops up every so often, generates a few options but never reaches a conclusion. So, the conversations continued, and we got family members and friends involved as we toyed with variants. I could be Nagamootoo professionally and change my name to Smith for everything else... too complicated. I could be Nagamootoo and my husband and any future kids could be Smith... but we all wanted to share the same family name. We could mesh our names and be Nagamith or Smootoo... definitely not, no explanation needed! This went on until there was only one remaining logical decision – he would change his name to Nagamootoo.

There were already two other people with the same surname as him in his relatively small

Introduction

company, so it quite appealed to him to have a more unique name. And he also appreciated that since any children we had would be born and brought up in the British culture, carrying a Mauritian surname would offer them an anchor to their heritage. For him, going against tradition and changing his name to mine wasn't a big deal. What's in a name, right? Well, it turns out there's a lot in a name which we hadn't fully accounted for.

When I told one of my friends, she stared at me in surprise and asked, 'How do his parents feel about him leaving the family?'

'What do you mean "leaving the family"? He's no less part of their family just because his name is changing,' I replied, shocked and annoyed at her attitude.

And here lies the fundamental flaw in our analysis. We had forgotten to take into consideration the significance of history, tradition and societal values. Think of all the gender-based symbols and expectations involved in marriage – the man proposing, the father giving away the bride, the bride leaving her family to be provided for by her husband while she cares for him and the children. The concept of marriage is steeped in patriarchy, power and inequity.

The Inclusion Mindset

When my husband told his work colleagues that he was changing his name to mine, a few of them made remarks like, 'I can see who wears the trousers in your relationship.' To us, our marriage was two people coming together as equals and joining each other's families in equal measure. Our choice of surname had no bearing on our perspective of each other's families or on how we acted or behaved within each family. To the western world, our choice of surname indicated a role reversal. The perception was that I now had more power and he was less of a man (in the traditional sense of being the provider for our family). My family was more dominant, and I had rejected entering his.

I share this story with you for two reasons. First, it is a reminder of the importance of history, culture and values in decision making. This doesn't mean that we would have altered anything about our choice of family name, but simply that it would have helped us better deliver the news and manage the expectations of our families if we had considered the wider perspective. Second, it is a reminder that challenging inequity and disrupting the status quo will inevitably lead to upset. Why? Because this is deeply uncomfortable and eats away at the core of who we are.

Introduction

The act of my husband changing his surname to mine challenged the patriarchy and inequity of marriage. We hadn't appreciated how much we were asking of our families – that they let go of this traditional concept and move beyond their discomfort to accept that our choice was actually a rebalancing of our roles in marriage that brought down the power structures embedded in the system and created a beautiful parity between two families. It was a lot to ask without an explanation or a guiding hand.

Similarly, leading inclusively is tough because you have to constantly challenge yourself to operate beyond discomfort. This means fighting back the urge to remain fixed in your mindset and hold on to an entrenched view of how right you are. It means being able to reflect and analyse where your beliefs, values and rules about life come from (historically, socially and culturally) and to accept that there are multiple perspectives and that what is 'right' may not always be clear. It means looking for and noticing the hidden and intangible inequities deep within our organizational structures and searching for a way forward that offers justice and fairness, even though outwardly it may look like sacrificing the power of those who currently have it. It means acknowledging that an imperfect system elevates some at the cost of others and that a redistribution of power will have consequences for all. And it means being continuously cognizant of your own emotions and the fears that inevitably arise when there is change and uncertainty, and pushing yourself to have brave new conversations that educate and expand your understanding of those who are different to you.

An inclusive leader has to be skilful, adept and well-practised in self-reflection. They must understand their 'Way of Being' – where their beliefs come from – and be able to respond within seconds in a way that embraces a view different from their own. That's no mean feat.

I've written this book because I witness the struggle that people face with embodying inclusion in daily life – not just clients and colleagues (working in the space of diversity, equity and inclusion (DEI) automatically opens up conversations you wouldn't typically have) but also friends and family. I am privileged to have connected with and shared learning spaces with thousands of leaders globally to help them unravel the knotty, complex tensions that DEI brings.

Throughout this book, I invite you to recognize where your own beliefs come from, and to embrace self-reflection and emotional discomfort as vital steps toward real inclusion. You will be challenged to explore

Introduction

your reactions, to notice your questions and to become aware of your own emotional triggers and worldviews.

Ultimately, I hope that you will use the self-insights you gain from considering your leadership to break down barriers for underrepresented people, create a culture that reinforces inclusive behaviour and actively build teams with a greater sense of belonging – to adopt, in fact, an inclusion mindset.

Day 1
Why inclusion feels hard

We've come a long way since discussions of diversity were purely around equal opportunity for all. It seems almost naive now, looking back, that we thought that simply by creating legislative anti-discrimination acts, a change in how we treat minority groups would ensue. First, because policies and laws don't offer the educational upskilling or attitudinal shift required for societal change. Second, because it assumes that those policing these rules are free of bias and willing to abide by the rules. Third, because it doesn't take into consideration the complex and often invisible ways discrimination plays out. For many organizations, conversations around diversity have had a narrow focus on gender (men and women), disability and perhaps ethnicity. Gradually, over the years, we have

Why inclusion feels hard

bravely expanded our exploration to race, religion, culture, sexual orientation, caste, neurodiversity, mental health, age and gender through a non-binary lens, to name a few.

In more recent years, work in this space has broadened beyond diversity to consider equity, inclusion and belonging, from looking at representation across diverse characteristics to assessing the bias deep within the foundations and structures of the systems we operate in (society, organizations, teams, etc) and how we create fairness and justice so everyone feels valued and able to contribute their unique perspectives.

The language used in these conversations has evolved too. For example, 'intersectionality', a term coined by civil rights activist Kimberlé Crenshaw back in 1989, has only recently come into common-use DEI vocabulary as we have begun to realize the importance of how different dimensions of diversity overlay each other and create a cumulative impact of discrimination and oppression for individuals.[1] Another term, 'gaslighting', has risen in use to describe the manipulative tactics sometimes leveraged by those in power to undermine minority individuals' perception of reality. Language helps us construct meaning, but it also creates scope for complex conversations, misinterpretation and misunderstanding. As injustices are given labels and therefore made real, people from marginalized and minority groups have felt more legitimacy to expect change.

But why are organizations large and small discussing how to create a more inclusive culture? Is it simply a desire to do the right thing, or to gain competitive advantage, or to access a broader talent pool, or to improve their bottom line? The work of developing an inclusion mindset can be hard, and few leaders will fully embrace it without at least one or more very compelling reasons.

Hitting the bottom line

There is significant research on the business case for diverse workplace representation and organizational inclusion. Most leaders need more than encouragement that 'it's the right thing to do' – they need hard evidence that it makes business sense.

In 2017, Boston Consulting Group surveyed employees in over 1,700 companies in eight countries and found a strong correlation between diversity of leadership teams and better innovation and financial performance.[2] They measured diversity across gender, age, nation or origin, career path,

Why inclusion feels hard

industry background and education. They found that companies with above-average diversity in leadership averaged 19% higher in innovation revenue compared to those with below-average diversity in leadership.

When individuals with diverse thoughts are brought together to solve problems, new and innovative ideas are more likely to come about. Professor Katherine Phillips spent her academic career researching diversity and the impact on decision making. In a 2014 article in *Scientific American*, she explains an earlier study looking at the impact of racial diversity in small groups. It found that the racially diverse groups significantly outperformed the groups with no racial diversity. Phillips explains: 'Being with similar others leads us to think we all hold the same information and share the same perspective. This perspective, which stopped the all-White groups from effectively processing the information, is what hinders creativity and innovation.'[3]

Of course, simply having greater diversity won't lead to positive business outcomes without an inclusive culture that embraces difference. In their Getting to Equal 2019 report, Accenture identify how a culture of equality drives employees' innovation mindset.[4] The key driver to innovation is people feeling like they are in an 'empowering environment' where they are trusted and have the freedom to be creative. With innovative leadership comes a greater ability to anticipate customer needs and preferences, leading to improved customer retention and growth.

The power of aligning products to diverse consumer needs is illustrated by the redesign of the England women's football team kit. After concerns raised by players about period leakage, Nike designed blue shorts with an integrated absorbent liner. Would this need have been identified otherwise? It probably would never have occurred to any of the male decision makers to ask. What are more homogeneous leadership teams and organizations missing simply because of their narrower perspective on the world?

Tenders for new work now often require evidence that DEI practice has been actively embedded in the organization. Companies with corporate social responsibility high on their agendas want supply chains with equal integrity and commitment to DEI. This is often where the business case hits home quickly.

Slightly less tangible is the impact of DEI work on employer brand and reputation. An organization's reputation is precious and directly impacts customer buying choices, whether people recommend and

Why inclusion feels hard

speak positively about the organization and whether they want to work there.

I believe that continuous analysis of the future through a DEI lens, and flexing to meet the changing demands, will be organizations' greatest asset. Short-sightedness has been the downfall of an endless number of companies that chose to stick with the status quo, and leaders who ignore Gen Z's (and more recently Generation Alpha's) workplace requirements for inclusion, belonging and representation are setting themselves up to fail.[5]

So, an inclusion mindset is undeniably good for business, but equally undeniably it can feel hard. Over the coming days we'll explore the discomfort associated with this work, and how to move beyond it.

So what? Over to you...

1. Where do you see business opportunities in becoming more inclusive?

Why inclusion feels hard

2. What assumptions have you made about DEI that might be outdated or incomplete?

3. How does your own experience shape the way you see others and engage with conversations about DEI?

Day 2
The lens we see through

If everyone agrees that inclusion is important, why is there so much discomfort around it?

The reality is that discomfort is an inevitable part of learning and change. Our journey toward true inclusion requires us to explore not only what we do, but also how we *are*. Today we'll explore the core idea that our values, emotions and experience fundamentally shape our worldview – our 'Way of Being' – and why recognizing this is essential for any leader aspiring to be truly inclusive.

Our 'Way of Being' shapes everything

Alan Sieler, founder and Director of the Ontological Coaching Institute, describes Way of Being as 'How we are at any point in time, and in particular... how we are observing and perceiving the world.'[6]

Our Way of Being is the lens through which we interpret everything that happens around us. It's a product of our upbringing, our culture, our lived experiences and the stories we tell ourselves about the world and our place in it. These stories become so familiar that we often mistake them for objective truth.

Notice that I've deliberately chosen the term 'Way of Being' rather than words such as 'type' or 'trait'. Whereas, linguistically, leadership type or trait sounds more fixed and ingrained, a person's Way of Being, based on their experience and observations of the world, is malleable and can change with self-understanding, curiosity and open-mindedness.

However, change is never easy. As psychiatrist Elisabeth Kübler-Ross demonstrated, change comes with inevitable waves of emotion: denial, anger, bargaining ('If only I had done it differently'), depression and acceptance.[7] Similarly, when you're working to expand or shift your Way of Being you may discover truths that are shocking and feel angry that your good intentions are being attacked, regretful as you realize past errors, sad as you uncover colleagues' stories of deep trauma and pain, and overwhelmed at the scale of change required, but also accepting of your role as an ally. Part of the work is noticing when you become emotionally triggered and how you show ongoing personal commitment to work through these moments with the goal of inclusion always in your consciousness.

Invisible realities

It's all too easy for us to assume that other people's experience of the world is the same as ours. So, if people apply grit and work hard as we have done, then they will reap the same rewards. Systems psychologist David Kantor explains that this assumption fails to consider the 'invisible reality' within the privacy of each person's mind.[8] In other words, our interpretation of what we see and hear is based on our own unique lens, past experiences, biases and flaws. We naturally don't have access to other people's invisible realities, but they are always present and always inform our relationships, what we communicate and our outcomes.

When it comes to talking about privilege, for example, we're asking people to accept that what they observe in the world, and therefore what is true to them, is no one else's truth but their own. It might come very close to someone else's truth, which is more likely to be the case if they share similar diversity characteristics and a similar cultural lens. But because of our unique invisible realities, it'll never be 100% the same.

Tomorrow we'll look at four specific Ways of Being that, in my experience, reflect the most common leadership approaches to inclusion work.

The lens we see through

 So what? Over to you…

1. Where might you be mistaking your perspective for 'the truth' rather than 'a truth'?

The Inclusion Mindset

2. When conversations about inclusion feel uncomfortable, what emotions show up for you?

The lens we see through

3. What assumptions do you make about how others experience the workplace or society?

Day 3
The four Ways of Being

In my work facilitating workshops around DEI, I've witnessed the struggle that people face with embodying inclusion in work and life, and in response I've developed the Beyond Discomfort® model.

I've realized that in order to be truly inclusive, leaders need to demonstrate a 'Receptiveness to Learn'. This is not just about learning what they need to do as an inclusive leader but about educating themselves on history and cultures different from their own and delving deeply into learning about themselves. This includes an openness to learning by doing, despite the fear of misstepping.

They also need to show a 'Willingness to Act', not just passively – by liking other people's woke comments, for instance – but by constantly

The four Ways of Being

dismantling the inequities around them and challenging themselves and their colleagues to promote inclusion at times when accepting the status quo would be far easier and more comfortable.

These two concepts – Receptiveness to Learn and Willingness to Act – are related continuums which make up the axes of the model, and the four quadrants reveal four Ways of Being: Disconcerted, Proof-Seeking, Cheerleading and Beyond Discomfort.

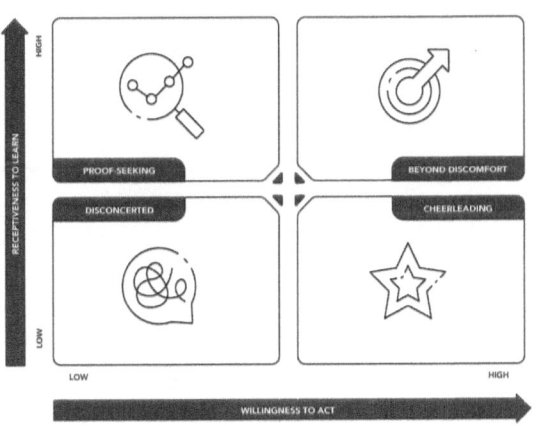

Disconcerted leaders:
- value the traditional principles of leadership – e.g. being assertive, taking action, having the answers

- believe in a meritocratic system where individuals are rewarded and achieve success based on talent
- believe DEI has gone too far, with minority individuals favoured to the detriment of majority individuals.

Proof-Seeking leaders:
- operate with curiosity for DEI and consider how they might adapt their leadership accordingly
- need to really understand what inclusive leadership looks like before they will shift from their default style
- feel agitated at the lack of clarity and complexity that inclusive leadership presents and, as a result, hold back from taking action.

Cheerleading leaders:
- believe the most respectful and fair leadership approach is to disregard differences between individuals
- believe in equality and treating everyone the same
- think that they already lead inclusively and see very little more they need to do.

The four Ways of Being

Beyond Discomfort leaders:
- are proactive in their learning approach to DEI and seek to deepen their awareness of societal power structures
- remain open to noticing how the world interacts with those who are different from them
- lean in to new and uncomfortable conversations to aid their inclusive endeavours.

This isn't about figuring out which of the four Ways of Being you are. Let's face it, the world already does a good enough job of putting people in boxes. Indeed, you may find that elements of two, three or all four resonate with you. Instead, it's intended as an accessible way of presenting different underlying values, beliefs and ways of observing the world, to help facilitate your own thinking and help you unpick the complexity in your own head.

For leaders, this model can be a powerful tool. Rather than expecting yourself or others to be 'naturally' inclusive, you start to see inclusion as a practice that is continually honed through moments of discomfort. It also creates more compassion for yourself and others. If someone is reacting defensively, it's likely they are in a state of discomfort. Rather than labelling them as resistant, ask: 'What might they feel threatened by?' and 'How can I create safety and invitation, rather than judgement?'

Let's look at all four quadrants briefly, before we turn to each in more detail over the coming days:

- The Disconcerted: low willingness to act, low receptiveness to learn. What you might hear: 'This feels unfair or exclusionary.'
- The Proof-Seeker: low willingness to act, high receptiveness to learn. What you might hear: 'Show me the evidence.'
- The Cheerleader: high willingness to act, low receptiveness to learn. What you might hear: 'I support this, but it doesn't seem fair not to treat people the same.'
- Beyond Discomfort: high willingness to act, high receptiveness to learn. What you might hear: 'I don't know, but I want to learn.'

Using the model

As a practical tool, the Beyond Discomfort® model invites ongoing self-inquiry and dialogue. Leaders can ask themselves: What language am I using

The four Ways of Being

about inclusion? What emotions arise when I am challenged? Am I acting, learning, both, or neither?

Teams and organizations can use the quadrants to map their collective culture: Where do we spend most of our time? What would it take to move towards deeper inclusion, both individually and together?

Note that no quadrant is inherently 'bad'. The model does not judge or rank but encourages honest reflection. Every leader will encounter discomfort; the difference is in how we choose to respond. Over the next chapters we'll explore each quadrant in turn. You can find a helpful questionnaire at www.beyond-discomfort.com/questionnaire to support your reflection.

So what? Over to you...

1. Which of the four Ways of Being resonates most with you right now, and why?

The four Ways of Being

2. Where do you notice yourself moving between these quadrants in different situations?

The Inclusion Mindset

3. How might your team or organization use the Beyond Discomfort® model to prompt honest reflection?

Day 4
The Disconcerted Leader

Those who are Disconcerted believe that fairness exists when everyone is treated in exactly the same way. To these leaders, DEI initiatives that focus on specific groups and exclude others are simply unfair.

However, this assumes that the world already operates fairly. What we often don't see is the daily adaptations that people from underrepresented groups make to fit in, or how the world treats them because of their difference. For example, people of different cultural backgrounds living in a culture where their 'face doesn't fit' the norm experience not just discrimination but additional cognitive load of trying to fit in and the emotional drain of not belonging.

Meritocracy... or mirrortocracy

To compensate for this bias, several organizations have taken positive action by setting quotas or clear targets to create parity of representation. That can leave people in the majority group feeling like they have less chance than before of getting a job or progressing in an organization. And that also seems unfair and often creates a feeling of resentment, with individuals feeling they need to defend what they have worked for.

Many Disconcerted Leaders have a fundamental belief in the concept of meritocracy – they consider workplaces to be fair and their success as due to their own hard work alone. What they have observed and experienced in the world has never indicated otherwise. Indeed, how could we ever quantify how much of their career success was down to hard work, ability and talent versus the positive bias deep in the system that favours people who look and speak like them?

Kristen Anderson, former Chief Diversity & Inclusion Officer at Barilla, helped unpick this complexity when she spoke to me on my podcast:

> A lot of people say, 'I don't believe in quotas or targets because I believe in meritocracy,'

The Disconcerted Leader

meaning 'I believe that we should promote or bring on board the most qualified people.' But let's be very clear, meritocracy is a wonderful theory, but it is not reality, because that means we have no biases. If I can evaluate every single candidate without any biases coming into my evaluation, I'm following meritocracy. But we're not robots and we do have biases. We tend to have an affinity bias – mirrortocracy. For example, I want to bring Kath on because she reminds me of myself when I was more junior in my career and I think she is the right person for the leadership team. I don't realize I have this bias, and so I'm not considering Luca, who is actually a more qualified candidate.[9]

There's nothing fundamentally wrong with a desire to be with someone who is comfortable and easy to talk to or work with. Why would you deliberately choose to spend the day with someone who is irritating because they have different views to you or someone who you need to expend a lot of energy on when you're in their presence? However, if we remain open to accepting that we have this tendency to be attracted to people similar to us, and that this influences our decision making, then it does call into question whether we achieved our promotions and job successes purely on the basis of talent alone. What if people have chosen you because you were similar to them? That's a pretty hard pill to swallow, right?

The dirty word: privilege

It can be enraging if someone implies you have 'privilege'. You might want to shout something like:

> How dare you tell me I haven't had to work to get to where I am, that I've had an easy life! I grew up poor, I was bullied for wearing hand-me-down clothes, I know what it feels like to be excluded, and I've made my way despite that!

Suggesting someone has privilege can feel like we're diminishing their success and that cuts deep at their pride. By default, if they have had an advantage that means other people have been disadvantaged, and both of these positions are invisible and impossible to measure.

We can't be blamed or made to feel guilty for our background, skin colour or gender, or for not experiencing every type of exclusion that exists. That expectation is neither right nor fair. However, once a leader becomes aware of a form of exclusionary behaviour, it is absolutely their responsibility to be alert to it and take action when they see it.

Note that privilege is socially constructed, and therefore as societal views have evolved over time, privilege has changed. There have been numerous figures and movements that accelerated a shift in privilege – for example, the suffragettes, Rosa Parks, the Stonewall riots, Nelson Mandela and Black Lives Matter. These moments in time saw a step change in awareness, perception and beliefs, demonstrating that group privilege is malleable, based on societal changes.

Privilege can also be gained or lost at an individual level. I see it as a continuum where you can move up and down depending on personal life choices. For example, I gained privilege (not consciously) through my choice of life partner – a White, middle-class man. But when he took my surname, he lost privilege. He now has the lifelong, painstaking task of correcting people when they misspell his surname! But there are other implications too. Research in 2003 by Marianne Bertrand of the University of Chicago and Sendhil Mullainathan of the Massachusetts Institute of Technology found that applicants with

White-sounding names were 50% more likely to be contacted for job interviews than those with typical Black names.[10]

The discomfort in acknowledging privilege exists can be present for anyone – whether in majority or minority groups. But by denying it, we further cement the power and inequity in our organizational systems.

The fear of change

Just like most of us revel in the feeling of grabbing a bargain, we also enjoy any advantages we have been offered (whether earned on not) in our lives. It's what we know, it makes for a good life, and we don't want to give it up.

Part of this fear is based on a zero-sum mindset, meaning that if someone is to prosper, someone else has to miss out. If people in majority groups have gained their successes as a result of taking away from those in the minority, surely in order to rebalance, we need to do the reverse? The problem with this reasoning, however, is that it depicts success in a fixed and absolute way.

As humans, we seem to automatically jump to the negative repercussions of change because it is taking us away from what we know. It's known as the 'status quo bias', which favours keeping things as they are rather than expending energy working out what change looks like. Yet, we have all experienced situations where a change we feared has led to new opportunities. Rather than viewing success as a fixed quantity that needs to be divided up, can we imagine success as something that can be cultivated and grown exponentially so that there is plenty for all?

Expanding this Way of Being

If you notice elements of a Disconcerted Way of Being within you, leverage your curiosity and find opportunities for group learning. Whether it's a group coaching circle or a group of leaders attending an inclusive leadership programme, open yourself to conversations where you can hear other people's experiences. In doing so, you may discover that colleagues you have sat next to for years don't necessarily experience the organization as you do. This is a helpful way of building your Receptiveness to Learn about yourself and DEI.

So what? Over to you...

1. What do you notice in yourself, both emotionally and physically, in reading about privilege?

2. When in your leadership have you felt threatened or unsettled by conversations about inclusion?

3. How might you stay present with your discomfort, rather than retreating or defending?

Day 5
The Proof-Seeker

Unlike the Disconcerted Way of Being, leaders who are Proof-Seeking don't necessarily feel threatened and sidelined in the DEI discussion. They want to learn more but have a reluctance to accept, without evidence, what is being described. So, while the top left-hand box in the Beyond Discomfort® model represents a high Receptiveness to Learn, Proof-Seeking leaders are also sense-making based on their established truths and what they observe as reality, and when the information doesn't stack up, they are more likely to disregard it, which creates a low Willingness to Act.

Both pressure and organizational expectations often make it hard for leaders to move away from what is known to them, what has made them successful and continues to work for them.

So those with a Proof-Seeking Way of Being are trying to make sense of DEI through their own lens of what is true and real for them. In psychology, this is known as an 'anchoring bias' – that is, the tendency to place more validity on the initial information we have (in this case, our personal experiences) and less on new information (other people's experiences). So, although those who are Proof-Seeking are curious to expand their understanding, they aren't necessarily accessing the information they need to do so.

Is it possible that the common scenario of White men progressing to the top of the organization is purely due to them being better at their jobs, or more committed to work, than any other demographic counterpart? Yes. Is it also likely that an organization designed by men will have processes and systems that favour people like them? Absolutely.

So, what needs to happen? Those in the majority groups who find themselves achieving higher levels of organizational status need to start actively interrogating the system in search of bias. For example, what are the diversity characteristics of those who make promotion decisions? Are behaviours typically displayed by those in the majority rewarded in the organization? What is the organizational attitude towards part-time, flexible and remote workers? Is this consistently applied in all areas of the organization, by every manager? For those with a Proof-Seeking Way of Being, it will be important to search for the evidence, as it's unlikely to be immediately apparent.

Fear of the unknown

The fear of the unknown stems from trying to imagine what our leadership might look like when we openly acknowledge things that we're not good at and ask others to help bridge the gap. It comes from stepping away from a world of binaries – right and wrong, good and bad, competent and incompetent – and not knowing what being somewhere in-between means. Not just what it means with regard to leadership behaviour, but also how people will perceive you if you start questioning yourself and saying that you might not have the answer. You have to believe that your vulnerability will show strength rather than weakness, which might go against what you have seen and known in leaders before you. Think of the scene in *Indiana Jones and the Last Crusade* when our hero has to bravely step off the cliff and believe that there is an invisible bridge to step onto. Inclusive leadership is a trust exercise like no other. You have to believe that another reality exists without experiencing it yourself.

And the only way to discover alternative truths is to be open-minded and curious, actively seeking to spend time with people who are different to you, listening to other perspectives and being willing to realign your own beliefs. It's a tall order. It might feel awkward to be with a group of people who have a very different view of the world. There's a feeling of discomfort that comes with not belonging and being a guest, and that's a feeling that many people in majority groups are not familiar with because they're used to having licence to be in a space and to share their opinions freely.

Expanding this Way of Being

If I'm honest, I have some Proof-Seeking in me. My training as a psychologist, coach and MBA has deliberately developed my skill for critical thinking and questioning, which makes me want to find evidence and inquire more deeply. It makes me good at my job. But in the early days it also led me to question the validity of other people's lived experiences when hearing them for the first time.

The Proof-Seeker

The privilege I have of working in the DEI space is that I am constantly being offered people's lived experiences. Of course, my sceptical inner voice still exists when I hear a story that doesn't resonate with my reality, but I am now much more practised at hearing it and turning down the volume.

Tuning in to your inner voice is essential as an inclusive leader. Notice what it's telling you about the people you come across in your daily life. Do this for a while and you'll be able to notice how quick you are at drawing conclusions compared to remaining open to finding out more. To start looking at this more deeply, it's important to first recognize that what we take as fact is purely based on our own lived experiences and that other realities exist that we are as yet unaware of. We can then start identifying our narratives and patterns and ultimately go on a journey to open ourselves up to new possibilities by catching our thoughts, challenging our thinking and changing our stories. This is a useful cognitive behavioural therapy technique that I find leaders can easily implement as a way of positively reframing their thoughts.

So what? Over to you...

1. Where are you afraid of 'not knowing', or appearing less competent?

The Proof-Seeker

2. What would become possible if you saw uncertainty as a strength?

3. Who can you reach out to this week to stretch any Proof-Seeking tendencies?

Day 6
The Cheerleader

The Cheerleader occupies the quadrant of the Beyond Discomfort® model marked by high Willingness to Act but low Receptiveness to Learning. Cheerleaders want to do the right thing. They are often the first to step forward, to publicly affirm the value of inclusion, to volunteer for initiatives or to celebrate diversity days.

Leaders with a Cheerleading Way of Being have a fundamental belief that being inclusive means treating everyone the same, with fairness and respect. They often state with confidence that they don't see colour or gender or difference of any kind. These beliefs are coming from a well-intentioned place, but sometimes the intention doesn't lead to the desired outcome. If the general principle is to treat everyone the same to avoid being pulled up for favouritism, it can actually lead to inequity.

Invisible inequities

'Equality' and 'equity' are words that are often used interchangeably, but there's an important distinction between them. Equality is what those who are Cheerleading believe represents fairness, because it means treating everyone exactly the same. It's certainly one of the best ways to avoid being taken to an employee tribunal: no leader can be criticized for favouritism if they adhere to equality.

Equity, on the other hand, is about treating people based on their individual needs and in consideration of the unique challenges or barriers that they face because of their diversity characteristics. Workplace inequity is often invisible, hidden in the depths of the organization's structures, processes and culture. An example would be job descriptions that require a level of qualification not actually necessary to be successful in the role, which limit opportunities for people from lower socio-economic backgrounds.

You may look at members of your team and at people across your organization and see plenty of diversity, which is an indication that we have come a long way in creating equal opportunity. That may be true, but diversity across the organization doesn't automatically mean that there is equity and inclusion, or that people feel like they belong. Those who are Cheerleading tend to assume that there is diversity in their team and in leadership positions because everyone has been treated the same – that is, their differences have not been acknowledged. But what if they achieved this *despite* being treated the same?

Inclusion is complex

When I talk about this to leaders who have a Cheerleading Way of Being, they often look at me as if I've asked them to pull a rabbit out of a hat: 'So what you're saying is that in order to lead inclusively, I have to treat people differently based on something that can't be measured or seen?!' In short, yes, that is what I'm asking. However, the inequities are only invisible because we haven't programmed our brains to look for them and we haven't created a safe space in our teams or organizations to open up the conversation.

This, of course, isn't a quick win and it takes effort (a lot of it). Life is already hugely complex and challenging. If, by Cheerleading, we can keep it simple and treat everyone in exactly the same way, that would limit our chance of error. However, the reality is that this approach leaves those who are Cheerleading more open to error. One of my workshop participants offered a helpful example: 'Not seeing colour is like saying to someone in a wheelchair, "I don't see wheels." But that means you haven't considered how they move around in the world, the challenges they face and how it's historically been used against them.'

The complexity of what being an inclusive leader requires can be overwhelming, and this also creates fear: of saying the wrong thing, of not effectively navigating the complexity. There have been numerous recent examples of public outcry as a result of someone making a polarizing comment on social media, often simply because of an unfortunate turn of phrase rather than a deliberate desire to be discriminatory. The implications of 'cancel culture' are both toxic and unhealthy, not just in terms of the punishment and ostracizing of a person for one error in language, but for the fear it generates in broader society and for leaders in organizations. Too often leaders simply become frozen in discomfort and navigate their way back to what they know best.

Expanding this Way of Being

So, what do you do with this discomfort?

Leaders who have a Cheerleading Way of Being should try to seek what psychologist Angela Duckworth calls 'grit' within themselves – 'passion and perseverance for very long-term goals'.[11] They have a solid foundation due to their existing motivation to enhance DEI, but they also need to accept when their current paths aren't serving their goals. Being able to let go of a deeply held belief system and start again, this time following a different course, is where this grit will really show through.

Those with a Cheerleading Way of Being have spent their lives and careers leading in ways that they felt were inclusive. If you recognize features of Cheerleading in yourself, reading this will likely have been uncomfortable for you, to say the least. You're not a bad leader because you sometimes hold this Way of Being. However, you might consider pressing the reset button on some of your existing beliefs about inclusion.

So what? Over to you…

1. Where might you have assumed that fairness means sameness?

2. Can you find an example of where equality and equity might differ in your team?

3. How might you begin to develop the grit necessary for sustaining inclusion work?

Day 7
Leading Beyond Discomfort

Now for the final quadrant of the model: Beyond Discomfort, where both Willingness to Act and Receptiveness to Learn are high.

Leaders who have a Beyond Discomfort Way of Being have broken free of society's traditional stereotypes of what a good leader should be. Their willingness to learn about themselves, their privilege and their beliefs and biases means they understand the lens through which they see the world is different to everyone else's. They are prepared to tune in to their inner voice and challenge any unfair judgements and assumptions they are making about other people. They are open to having new conversations and, even though they might not fully understand every aspect of what they are told, their high Willingness to Act equitably and inclusively means they are prepared to be guided by what others tell them. They recognize the personal risks that showing this vulnerability carries and the often intense discomfort that this path takes and they take it anyway.

This doesn't mean that leaders with a Beyond Discomfort Way of Being won't at times be exclusionary. There will always be gaps in knowledge, understanding and analysis of actions. The difference, though, is that they are more likely to spot gaps, more practised at navigating the discomfort that this presents and more adept at accepting the change they need to make in themselves and in their leadership. They have adopted, in short, the inclusion mindset.

Courage

Challenging the system, whether it's one person or an organization, is scary, and often there is a lot at stake. Imagine you're a senior leader attending an industry dinner event with important clients. Wine is on tap and the drunken behaviour includes inappropriate sexual comments about the waitresses. What do you do? The discomfort often plays out on two levels: first, trying to find the best form of words to address the behaviour; and, second, the internal struggle of potentially jeopardizing current and future business relationships. It takes courage to say something, which will likely mean you will stick out and be on the receiving end of aggrieved and possibly aggressive people who will simply push you out of 'the circle' – you no longer belong because you 'can't take a joke'. It is also a developed skill to be able to select the most effective method to challenge in a given scenario.

However you go about it, challenging exclusionary behaviour always involves discomfort and therefore always requires courage. As Brené Brown puts it: 'The greatest barrier to courageous leadership is not fear – it's how we respond to our fear.'[12]

Perhaps the greatest courage is to face the uncomfortable truths about ourselves: that we hold biases and unknowingly act on them, that we make negative judgements about people who are different from us, that at least part of our success is due to our background, that we are not always good people.

Inclusive leaders need to sit with the constant discomfort that this awareness brings and resiliently continue down the never-ending path of deep inner work. And what sets these leaders apart is that they have a willingness to share their discoveries – both about themselves and what they notice in the world – as they live them, with openness, honesty and raw vulnerability. They allow people to witness their struggles or lack of understanding first-hand, thereby creating permission for others to do the same.

Supporting this Way of Being

Consistently having a Beyond Discomfort Way of Being is tough. Think about everything that's discussed in this chapter – this is someone who has the courage to call in or call out exclusionary behaviour, who can look deeply at the world around us and see the grim reality that it holds and also manage the inner tension of their contribution to this and be able to show their vulnerability in service of learning. They must be able to critically evaluate their pre-existing beliefs and values continuously and with an open mind that allows them to reassess their truths. Simultaneously, they need to reconcile their discoveries with their sense of self, noticing how this is evolving through acknowledging both the good and not so good aspects of who they once were, and still might be.

Even if this style of leadership comes naturally to you, in this fast-paced, always-on culture we are now living in, it is so easy to solely focus on tasks and deadlines and forget to pause. This pause is crucial to supporting an inclusive leader – first, because only then can we truly listen to our inner voice and start challenging its assumptions; and, second, because it offers us space to dissect the meaning behind what we have noticed in ourselves.

Pause can come in many different forms: meditation, grounding, physical exercise, yoga, going for a walk, quiet reflection. Use the time to reflect on moments of discomfort when perhaps you're trying to avoid an inner struggle or uncertainty related to DEI.

Alongside this independent support you can offer to yourself, you can also build collective resilience through finding a few people in your organization who are on the same leadership endeavour as you. You don't have to work through this complexity on your own.

So what? Over to you...

1. When have you chosen comfort over courage recently, and what might that have cost others?

2. How can you show others that learning out loud is safe and encouraged?

3. What support for this work could you put in place this week?

Day 8
Building an inclusive culture

Imagine an organization where the chief executive and top team are all leading Beyond Discomfort. They offer safe spaces for people to share their perspectives, inquire with genuine curiosity to learn about employees' different experiences, are open to dismantling processes and systems so they are more equitable, actively bring in diverse talent that reflects their market, are transparent about what they don't get quite right and hold managers accountable when they don't see the same. What an incredible organization to work for – and what a competitive advantage!

Sadly, that's not how it usually works. More commonly, the leader finds someone in the organization who has a passion for DEI (typically who identifies with a marginalized group) and squeezes it into their day job, or they create a new DEI position or hand it to the HR lead (because DEI is about people). This individual then has responsibility to increase representation across the organization, even though this isn't something one person can achieve. It's clear to everyone that this is just lip service, and it invokes an unhealthy cynicism. And because the focus is on awareness-raising rather than changing behaviours or mindsets, progress is minimal and any early momentum is lost.

Today we'll look at the fundamentals of taking an organization Beyond Discomfort, which stems from a collective and genuine desire to achieve inclusion across all senior leaders together with a clear, data-led DEI strategy.

Go deep, tackle culture

The journey towards an organization Beyond Discomfort must start with the top team because they set the tone for the organization's culture. Not just one or two members, but all of them.

They need to be collectively willing to peel back every layer of the organization to see what is below the surface, no matter how shocking the discoveries.

Building an inclusive culture

They need to recognize how the current systems, processes and policies have historically served certain types of people (including themselves) more than others and seek to make the necessary changes. They need to all be aligned on the view that DEI is core to their business performance so that, even during times of crisis, it never falls off their board meeting agenda. They need to expend time and effort, both individually and collectively, to make their organizational DEI commitments reality and empower others to do the same.

And all this work needs to be visible to the whole organization. Where the aspiration is clear and consistently role modelled by senior leaders, it inspires change throughout.

Creating champions

You'll find that many employees are passionate about DEI and want to get involved in the work. Not only is it important for the organization to recognize and utilize this untapped energy, but I'd also say cultural change can't happen without these individuals. Creating a DEI committee that is sponsored by an active senior leader is a great way to establish a call to action. It can be open to anyone in the organization and can have the dual purpose of creating space for people to share and discuss DEI topics while also delivering the organization's DEI strategy. Make sure there are clear delivery goals with a mechanism to report progress to senior leadership. This is key to sustaining engagement, as people will feel energized by the visibility of their work.

You might also consider identifying DEI champions or ambassadors: people on the ground, in each office location, who can observe, respond to DEI questions or requests for support, and collectively offer a sense of the wins to be celebrated and challenges to be worked on. If so, make sure you put in place:

- a clear profile for this role with defined responsibilities
- an executive sponsor who meets with the champions regularly and then discusses themes with the leadership team
- DEI training to build the knowledge and confidence of individuals in the role
- engagement with the champions' line managers so that the role isn't just an add-on
- some way to reward the champions for the additional duties (doesn't have to be financial, might involve giving them visibility

with senior leaders, enabling them to attend high-profile DEI events, formalizing their role so they can add it to their LinkedIn page and CV...).

Direction and transparency

Any culture transformation programme must have a vision of the future and a strategy to get there. There is only one place to start, and that's with a DEI strategy that is based on organizational data and has a robust narrative sitting behind it that everyone understands and supports.

In my experience, the key to success has always started with the CEO delivering an open and transparent message to their staff about what the current data shows. This is powerful because it shows vulnerability in stating what the organization isn't good at, builds credibility through owning the data and creates a psychological contract with employees in terms of its commitment to learning more and doing something about it. Then we can begin the work.

Since a DEI strategy should be grounded in the specific needs of the organization, we begin with surveys, analysing the experiences of everyone who works there. Data often reveals uncomfortable truths, and executive leaders can respond with denial and defensiveness or inquisitiveness and embracingness. Owning the data and sharing it across the organization will be uncomfortable. But transparency is crucial for trust and belief, and the sustained action that follows is key to dispelling cynicism and engendering collective momentum to change.

Hearts and minds

Policies, targets and processes can take you only so far. True inclusion lives in the attitudes and behaviours of people at every level. That means engaging not just the intellect but also the emotions – helping people feel the 'why' behind the work. Storytelling ignites our imagination and enhances empathy. When we hear someone's story, we walk in their shoes and therefore feel their pain.

For those with a Cheerleading or Proof-Seeking Way of Being, this stark evidence of a different reality and different truth is vital. It encourages all staff to lean in to the discomfort of seeing someone else's pain through perspective-taking and empathy. For those who have a fear of the unknown, it provides concrete evidence of inequity by opening a small window into someone's daily struggle to fit in. It motivates and inspires people who have a fear of complexity to set aside their concern of saying or doing the wrong thing, because the current state of play is far from good enough. And it signposts to all who work in an organization that it is open to and encouraging of uncomfortable conversations around typically taboo diversity topics.

Going global

For multinational organizations, inclusion cannot be a one-size-fits-all export from headquarters. Local cultural contexts shape how inequity is experienced, and strategies must be tailored accordingly. In some countries, conversations about certain identities may be legally restricted or socially taboo; in others, specific groups may be marginalized in ways that are invisible from afar.

This requires both humility and curiosity from leaders. Rather than imposing a global template, invite local teams to co-create inclusion goals that align with their reality. Provide resources and frameworks but allow flexibility in how they are applied. And ensure that global decision-making bodies themselves reflect geographic diversity, so that perspectives from different regions genuinely shape strategy.

Taking a stand

Taking a stand for DEI needs to expand to each touchpoint the organization has. Where do you draw the line in working with suppliers or clients that display values counter to DEI?

An organization Beyond Discomfort recognizes that its historical supplier or client base may not align to their DEI values and is willing to hold them to account even if it means losing business. In expressing to the world what they stand for and taking action to demonstrate it, organizations will attract clients that hold DEI of equal importance. These organizations are growing in number and are actively pursuing an ethical supply chain. Despite the short-term risk and uncertainty, the longer-term gain is a value-aligned organization that can send a powerful message to its employees, enhancing their trust and establishing accountability.

Leaders need to be prepared to make risky, uncomfortable decisions to stand by their DEI values, even if that means challenging stakeholders, clients and suppliers or sharing their views publicly. It takes time, effort and continuous reinforcement, but it is possible – and it is definitely worth it.

So what? Over to you…

1. In what ways does your organization demonstrate that DEI is a core business priority?

2. How open are you to sharing uncomfortable data, even when it might reflect poorly on the organization?

3. If your organization had to take a stand on a social issue tomorrow, how could it ensure it was prepared?

Day 9
Facing the future of work

The pace of change in our world is relentless. New technologies, shifting demographics, evolving societal expectations and global crises are transforming how we live and work. For organizations, this brings both uncertainty and opportunity. Navigating the future of work through an inclusive lens is no longer optional – it's essential for survival.

Why the future demands inclusion

The next decade will see accelerating disruption across industries. The good news is that inclusion offers resilience in the face of disruption. A workforce with diverse perspectives is better equipped to anticipate challenges, adapt to change and spot opportunities. Inclusive leaders can navigate uncertainty with empathy, maintain trust during upheaval and keep teams engaged even when the path ahead is unclear.

The same applies at an organizational level. Those that build inclusive cultures now will have the strong foundations needed to withstand shocks – whether technological, environmental or political. Without that foundation, cracks will appear quickly when disruption hits.

Technology and equity

The World Economic Forum predicts that by 2028, 44% of workers will have to gain new skills and there will be a loss of 83 million jobs.[13] As AI transforms workplaces, the jobs that are more likely to disappear are lower-paid manual and clerical jobs and those that involve repetitive tasks. The risk, from a DEI perspective, is that this will extend the socio-economic divide even more unless we find a way to reskill these workers.

But it's not all downsides. There will be new job growth and opportunities on an individual level to rapidly upskill and pivot to emerging market needs. On a macro level, organizations will need creative and diverse thinking more than ever to evolve with the marketplace and remain relevant. Leaders will continuously need to make rapid and tough decisions about the future of their organizations, shifting strategic focus, automating where possible, streamlining for efficiencies and upskilling in new areas. Critically, throughout this, there will be a need for care, empathy, active listening and inclusive leadership to maintain a positive workplace culture in the face of vulnerability and fear in such a turbulent and unsettling time.

The unity and solidarity that inclusion and belonging bring is what will offer organizations the strength to navigate through the current and impending disruptions.

Demographic change and generational shifts

In 2025, Generation Z made up around 27% of the workforce, forecast to increase to 31%, the largest generation in the job market, by 2035.[14] This is the first generation to have grown up entirely in the digital age, with expectations shaped by constant connectivity, global awareness and rapid information exchange. They are more likely to prioritize social and environmental responsibility over salary, to expect representation across all identities and to seek lattice-style careers over traditional hierarchies.

Unless those at the top are willing to step away from their belief system and embrace an inclusion mindset by taking Gen Z's perspective on work into account, this younger generation are quite prepared to exit via the nearest escape route and find somewhere that will. This can feel unsettling to leaders from older generations, for whom loyalty meant staying the course and accepting established norms.

Generational diversity within the workforce can be a strength, bringing together experience, innovation and varied perspectives. Yet it requires leaders to move Beyond Discomfort – to challenge assumptions about what commitment looks like, and to design cultures where multiple working styles and priorities can coexist.

So what? Over to you…

1. Where could an inclusion mindset strengthen your future readiness?

Facing the future of work

2. Where will your organization most benefit from diverse thinking over the next decade?

3. What changes in culture, voice or power are required in your organization to attract and retain the younger generation of talent?

Day 10
Your inclusion mindset journey

As busy leaders, we have little time to reflect on how our deeply held values and beliefs influence how we interpret the world or why our emotions are activated when something jars with us. When it comes to DEI, we tend to be more aware of how the enhanced focus on diversity in our organization, and in society more generally, sparks a series of thoughts and questions:

- 'This doesn't make sense.'
- 'It isn't fair. I can't help my privilege.'
- 'I don't understand why we're meant to see people's differences.'
- 'What exactly should I be saying or doing to be more inclusive?'
- 'What happens if I say or do the wrong thing?'

So, in the end, the uncertainty, fears and discomfort evoked by DEI can actually limit our learning and action.

Organizations wanting to make progress in DEI naturally want their leaders to take active roles. For example, they might be a sponsor of an employee resource group, support a positive action programme or participate in a panel discussion at an all-staff event. But, if leaders are operating with elements of the Disconcerted, Proof-Seeking or Cheerleading Ways of Being, they will likely show less energy for the work, and culture change will be much slower as a result. I hope I have encouraged you to reconsider your starting point – inclusive leadership involves deep psychological work that is hugely uncomfortable but shouldn't be avoided.

I created the Beyond Discomfort® model to help you reflect on your way of observing the world. Remember that the purpose isn't for you to find your 'fit', but to support a deeper process of self-reflection on how your own life story, belief systems and personal circumstances shape your response to DEI. I believe that we'll only be able to achieve equity and inclusion once most leaders lean into this. I realize, of course, that not everyone will want to or, indeed, have the capacity to do so. That's OK – I didn't write this book to 'convert' you or get you to do something you don't want to do. But if you find you are resisting or questioning your organization's DEI work, then I hope this book has provoked thought and understanding as to why. If all leaders took this initial step, I believe we would find it much easier to enter into healthy and open discussions to unravel the complexity and find a path together.

The way ahead

I offer here a few reminders of some of the key takeaways from this book. You may have had numerous other moments of provocation and learning from your 6-minute exploratory writing sprints, all of which are valuable and which you should hang on to, reflect on and use to guide your leadership. I am always happy to hear about these, so please reach out and share.

- DEI work, and in particular creating equity, can cause people with majority characteristics to feel sidelined, guilty for their privilege and unfairly treated. If you feel this way, it's important that you recognize this and reflect on what specifically evokes this.

The Inclusion Mindset

- Believing in a meritocratic system isn't realistic given the biases we all carry and our human desire to connect to people like us. While it may be deeply uncomfortable, you may want to spend time revisiting your narrative about your earned successes in life and consider how your diversity characteristics may have influenced your experiences.
- It can be tough to hear other people's truths and confusing if you haven't seen any evidence of them. It's important to create space for people to share their truths with you, recognize the emotions that are evoked in you when they do and use this new knowledge to shape your leadership.
- Strength in leadership doesn't come from having all the answers, but from showing awareness that you don't. Reflecting on your definition of leadership and allowing the collective wisdom of other people's realities to inform your perspective and decision making is key to inclusion.
- DEI holds many paradoxes, one of which is that we need to see people's differences for them to feel included. Discomfort is

Your inclusion mindset journey

inevitably present when we open ourselves to seeing people's differences, because we suddenly become aware of invisible inequities that we may have unintentionally contributed to. Actively seeking out inequities and supporting work to dismantle systemic bias is vital to creating change.

- Inclusive leaders don't have to permanently operate Beyond Discomfort – this would be unrealistic. However, they should practise discomfort regularly, noticing when their emotions and fears get the better of them and considering why. This continual process of self-reflection, navigating emotions so that you move into more productive places, and being open to learning by doing (despite the potential mistakes) is what will set you apart as a truly inclusive leader.
- To achieve organizational inclusion, most or all leaders need to be willing to practise discomfort, both individually and collectively, in their decision making. This takes organizational vulnerability to another level by opening up new, uncomfortable conversations internally, being transparent

about where the current issues are and publicly showing allyship. This maturity takes a significant amount of work, investment and time, but the benefits for employee well-being and for the bottom line and organizational sustainability are well worth it.

Your inclusion mindset journey

✏️ So what? Over to you...

1. What's been most challenging to you as you've worked through this book?

2. What's been most exciting?

Your inclusion mindset journey

3. What changes will you make in your leadership that will reflect an inclusion mindset?

Conclusion

As you have seen throughout these ten days, developing an inclusion mindset is about more than learning the right words or implementing a set of initiatives. It is about shifting your Way of Being: noticing the beliefs you hold, understanding where they come from and being willing to see the world through perspectives different from your own. This requires patience, humility and an openness to being changed by what you learn.

You will not always get it right. There will be times you step back into comfort, moments when fear or habit pulls you towards the familiar. That is not failure; it is part of the process. The question is not whether you will face discomfort again, but how you will choose to respond when you do.

The impact of your new Way of Being extends beyond your immediate sphere. It influences how your teams operate, how your organization evolves and how the people you lead experience their work and their worth. It ripples outward to customers, partners and communities.

Conclusion

In a world that will continue to change in unpredictable ways, the leaders who will endure are those who can adapt without losing their principles. Inclusion is a foundation for resilience, innovation and trust.

The journey is lifelong, and it belongs to all of us. Thank you for travelling this far – and for your willingness to go further.

Endnotes

[1] K. Crenshaw, 'Demarginalizing the intersection of race and sex: A Black feminist critique of antidiscrimination doctrine, feminist theory and antiracist politics' in *University of Chicago Legal Forum*, 1989 (1), Article 8 (1989). Available from: https://chicagounbound.uchicago.edu/uclf/vol1989/iss1/8

[2] https://www.bcg.com/publications/2018/how-diverse-leadership-teams-boost-innovation

[3] K.W. Phillips, 'How diversity makes us smarter' in *Scientific American* (1 October 2014). Available from: www.scientificamerican.com/article/how-diversity-makes-us-smarter/

[4] Accenture, 'Getting to Equal 2019: Creating a Culture that Drives Innovation' in Accenture (2019). Available from: www.accenture.com/content/dam/accenture/final/a-com-migration/thought-leadership-assets/accenture-equality-equals-innovation-gender-equality-research-report-iwd-2019.pdf

[5] GWI, *Generation Alpha: The Real Picture* (2022).

[6] A. Sieler, *Coaching to the Human Soul: Ontological Coaching and Deep Change,* Volume 1 (2003).

[7] E. Kübler-Ross, *On Death and Dying* (1969).

Endnotes

[8] D. Kantor and S. Hill, 'Working with an invisible reality' in *Training Journal* (August 2014). Available from: www.dialogix.co.uk/wp-content/uploads/2014/10/TJ-AUGUST-2014-low.17-20.pdf

[9] Quotes from podcast discussions have been lightly edited for clarity and context while attempting to be true to the original work. All podcast episodes were recorded during 2020–23, and they can be found at www.avenirconsultingservices.com/podcast

[10] M. Bertrand and S. Mullainathan, 'Are Emily and Greg More Employable than Lakisha and Jamal? A Field Experiment on Labor Market Discrimination' in *National Bureaux of Economic Research* (2003). Available from: www.nber.org/system/files/working_papers/w9873/w9873.pdf

[11] A. Lee Duckworth, 'Grit: The power of passion and perseverance', TED (April 2013). Available from: www.ted.com/talks/angela_lee_duckworth_grit_the_power_of_passion_and_perseverance

[12] B. Brown, Dare to Lead hub. Available from: https://brenebrown.com/hubs/dare-to-lead

[13] World Economic Forum, *Future of Jobs Report 2023: Insight Report May 2023* (2023). Available from: www3.weforum.org/docs/WEF_Future_of_Jobs_2023.pdf

[14] www.zurich.com/media/magazine/2022/how-will-gen-z-change-the-future-of-work

Enjoyed this?
Then you'll love…

 *Beyond Discomfort* by Nadia Nagamootoo

Business Book Awards 2025 Finalist

getAbstract International Book Award 2024 Finalist

'An excellent, example-rich and immediately practical book which will no doubt stay close to hand and dog-eared with use for years to come.' Dr Pippa Grange Psychologist and Author of *Fear Less*

Talk to anyone about Diversity, Equity and Inclusion (DEI) and it sparks a whole range of emotions. Why? Because DEI, at its very core, is about values and beliefs, and it's about change. So it is no surprise then, that despite putting in place a DEI strategy and multiple initiatives, so many organizations get stuck.

Enjoyed this? Then you'll love...

Beyond Discomfort reveals a new model of inclusive leadership, which describes four belief systems and associated emotional responses to DEI.

Discover:

- real life stories and expert insights to deepen your understanding of why DEI is so knotty and complex
- self-understanding and new perspectives to better connect with your learned leadership values and beliefs
- reflective questions, practical tools and activities to help develop your inclusive practice.

Nadia Nagamootoo is a Chartered Psychologist, accredited coach, MBA and Founder of Avenir, a DEI consultancy. Through her multiple keynotes and popular podcast show, Why Care?, Nadia has become a profound thought leader in DEI, guiding organizations on an accelerated path to creating inclusion and belonging.

Other *6-Minute Smarts* titles

 *Beating Burnout* (based on *The Burnout Bible* by Rachel Philpotts)

 *Building Great Teams* (based on *Workshop Culture* by Alison Coward)

 *Collaborate Better* (based on *Collabor(h)ate* by Deb Mashek PhD)

 *Customer Success Essentials* (based on *The Customer Success Pioneer* by Kellie Lucas)

 *Do Change Better* (based on *How to be a Change Superhero* by Lucinda Carney)

 *Find Your Confidence* (based on *Coach Yourself Confident* by Julie Smith)

 *Find Your Purpose* (based on *The Purpose Handbook* by Eloise Skinner)

 *Get That Promotion* (based on *Getting On* by Joanna Gaudoin)

 *Grow Your Product Business* (based on *Tame Your Tiger* by Catherine Erdly)

 *How to be Happy at Work* (based on *My Job Isn't Working!* by Michael Brown)

 *How to Get to Know Your Customer* (based on *Do Penguins Eat Peaches?* by Katie Tucker)

 *The Listening Leader* (based on *The Listening Shift* by Janie Van Hool)

 *Love Your Job* (based on *WorkJoy* by Beth Stallwood)

Managing Big Teams (based on *Big Teams* by Tony Llewellyn)

Mastering People Management (based on *Mission: To Manage* by Marianne Page)

No-Fluff Soft Skills (based on *Soft Skills, Hard Results* by Anne Taylor)

No Nonsense PR (based on *Hype Yourself* by Lucy Werner)

Present Like a Pro (based on *Executive Presentations* by Jacqui Harper)

Reimagine Your Career (based on *Work/Life Flywheel* by Ollie Henderson)

Sales Made Simple (based on *More Sales Please* by Sara Nasser Dalrymple)

The Speed Storytelling Toolkit (based on *Exposure* by Felicity Cowie)

Stay Focused (based on *Attention!* by Rob Hatch)

Write to Think (based on *Exploratory Writing* by Alison Jones)

Look out for more titles coming soon! Visit www.practicalinspiration.com for all our latest titles.

www.ingramcontent.com/pod-product-compliance
Lightning Source LLC
Chambersburg PA
CBHW031438210526
45464CB00005B/2253